SING IN THE BARBERSHOP QUARTET
VOLUME 5

# CHRISTMAS COLLECTION

T0084243

Beginning pitches on the CD are the root (tonic) of the song's key.

ISBN 978-1-4803-5234-6

HAL•LEONARD®
CORPORATION

7777 W. BLUEMOUND RD. P.O. BOX 13819 MILWAUKEE, WI 53213

Visit Hal Leonard Online at
**www.halleonard.com**

## CONTENTS

# Do You Hear What I Hear

Arrangement by
JOE LILES

Words and Music by NOEL REGNEY
and GLORIA SHAYNE

# (There's No Place Like)
# Home for the Holidays

Arrangement by RUSS FORIS
and BURT SZABO

Words and Music by AL STILLMAN
and ROBERT ALLEN

10

# I'll Be Home for Christmas

**Arrangement by
S P E B S Q S A**

*Words and Music by* **KIM GANNON**
*and* **WALTER KENT**

# It's Beginning to Look Like Christmas

**Arrangement by**
**WILLIS A. DIEKEMA**

By MEREDITH WILLSON

# Let It Snow! Let It Snow! Let It Snow!

Arranged by
JOE LILES

Words by SAMMY CAHN
Music by JULE STYNE

18

you'll real-ly hold me tight, _____ all the way home I'll be

warm. _____ Mm _____
warm. _____ Mm _____
warm. The fire is slow-ly dy-ing and my

dear, we're still good-bye-ing. But as long as you love me

so, _____ Let it snow! _____ Let it snow! _____ Let it

snow! Let it snow! Let it snow! _____

*rit.*

Let it snow! _____

*From MAME*

# We Need a Little Christmas

Arrangement by
**DAVE BRINER**

Music and Lyric by
**JERRY HERMAN**

**Verse**

in a hur - ry. So haul out the hol - ly.

Put up the tree be - fore my spir - it falls _____ a - gain.

**Fill**

Fill up the stock - ing. I may be

Fill

Fill

rush - ing things, but deck the halls _____ a - gain

**Chorus 2**

now. _____ For I've

23

*From the Motion Picture Irving Berlin's HOLIDAY INN*

# White Christmas

**Arrangement by**
**MAC HUFF**

**Words and Music by**
**IRVING BERLIN**

25

26

*Optional cut to measure 57*

# Little Saint Nick

**Arrangement by
JON NICHOLAS**

**Words and Music by BRIAN WILSON
and MIKE LOVE**

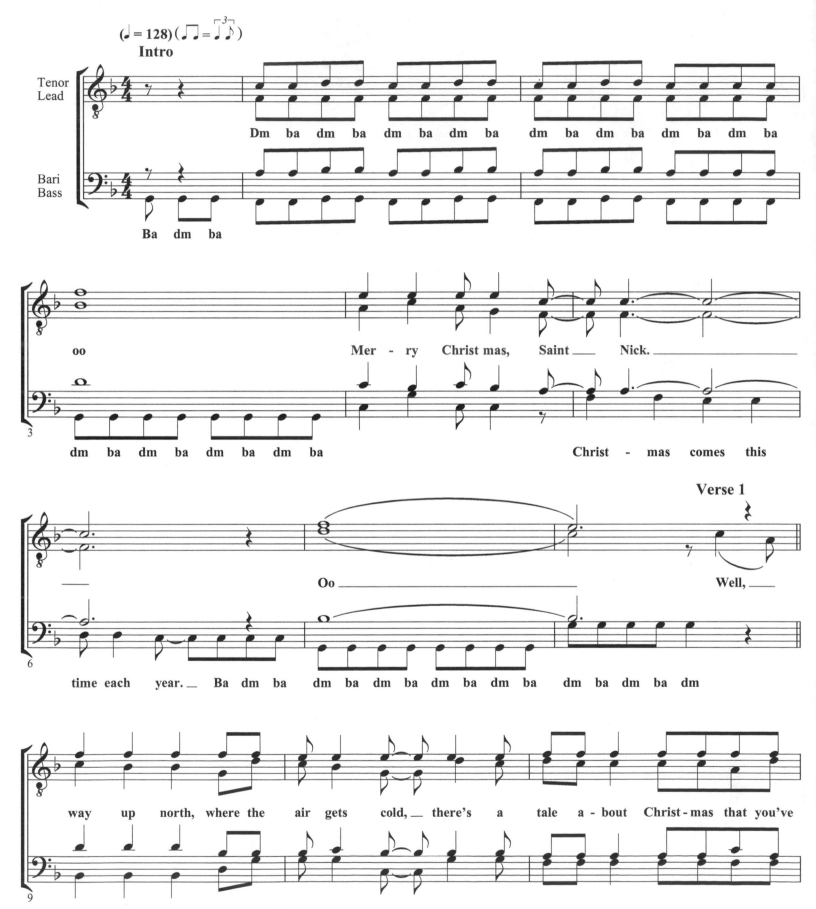

30

Chorus 2

San - ta hits the gas, man, just watch her peel. ____ It's the lit - tle Saint Nick, lit - tle Nick. ____

Saint Nick. It's the lit - tle Saint Nick, lit - tle Saint Nick. Nick. ____

A -

**Interlude**

Run, run, rein - deer, ____ run, run, rein - deer,

run, ba dm ba dm ba dm ba dm ba run, ba

whoa, ____ run, run, rein - deer, ____

dm ba dm ba dm ba dm ba run, ba dm ba dm ba dm ba dm ba

**Verse 3**

run, run, rein - deer. And haul - in' through the snow at a

run. He don't miss no one.

**Chorus 3**

32